C000258269

Rock Pool to Rainforest

Anita Ganeri

Explorer Challenge

Find out how this animal keeps cool ...

OXFORD
UNIVERSITY PRESS

Contents

What is a Habitat? 4

Seashore 6

Rainforest 10

Desert 14

Ocean 18

Woodland 22

City and Garden 26

Human Habitats 29

Glossary and Index 30

Look Back, Explorers 31

What is a Habitat?

A habitat is the home of a plant or animal. Plants and animals live in habitats where there is the food and shelter that they need.

Some habitats are huge.

My habitat is the Arctic. It is cold and icy all year round!

4

Some habitats are tiny. These tiny habitats are part of bigger habitats. The tiny habitats are called microhabitats.

My microhabitat is among the weeds that grow in a pond.

Let's take a look at some habitats and microhabitats around the world.

Seashore

A seashore is where the sea meets the land. Once or twice a day, the sea flows on to the land. Then it flows back out again. The seashore is a habitat for many creatures and plants. Some of them can live both in the water and on the land.

A seashore can be rocky or sandy. Sand is made from smashed-up rock, shells and coral.

Shallow waters

Oystercatchers live on the seashore. They have long legs for **wading** in the shallow water. They use their long beaks to open shells and eat the creatures inside.

Oystercatchers eat **cockles** and mussels. They also eat worms.

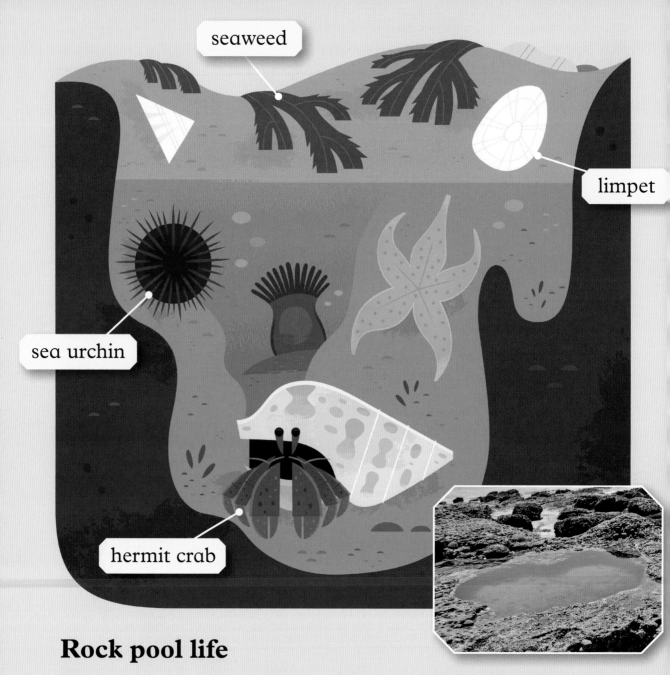

seaweed

limpet

sea urchin

hermit crab

Rock pool life

Rock pools are microhabitats on the seashore. Hermit crabs live in rock pools. Plants like seaweed, and animals like sea urchins and limpets live in rock pools too.

In the sand

Some seashore animals live in the sand under the surface. Lugworms dig U-shaped burrows. As they dig, they push out little piles of sand. These piles are left on the surface, and you can spot them all over the beach.

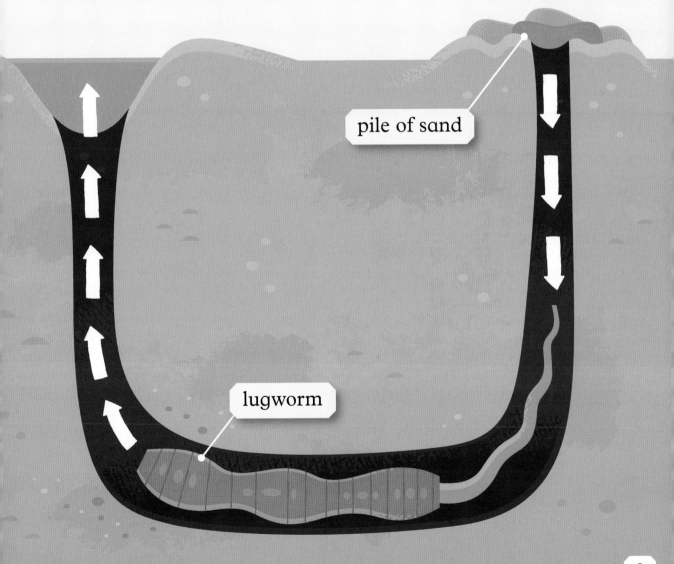

pile of sand

lugworm

Rainforest

Rainforests are large forests where it rains almost every day. They can be hot and sticky. They are a habitat for millions of plants and animals. More creatures live in rainforests than in any other habitat on Earth.

A single rainforest tree may be home to hundreds of kinds of beetle.

Jungle shadow

Jaguars live in the Amazon Rainforest. They hunt for deer, monkeys and even crocodiles to eat.

My spotty fur helps me to hide in the shadows of the trees.

Jaguars hide in the shadows and then pounce on their prey with their sharp claws. Their claws are good for climbing trees, too.

Pools made from leaves

Bromeliads (*say* brom-ee-lee-ads) are rainforest plants that grow on tree branches. Rain collects in the middle of their leaves. These pools of rainwater are microhabitats for some frogs. They carry their tadpoles to the pools of water. The tadpoles feed on insects and plants until they grow into frogs.

Bromeliad leaves have tiny scales that collect water from the air.

My green fur helps me to hide from **predators**.

Furry home

Sloths live in rainforests. The fur of a sloth is a microhabitat for **fungi** (*say* fun-gee), moths and beetles. Tiny green plants, called algae (*say* al-gee), also live on the sloth's fur and turn it green.

Desert

Deserts are the driest places on Earth. They can be extremely hot in the daytime, and freezing cold at night. Deserts may look empty but they are home to an amazing number of animals and plants.

In some deserts, no rain falls for years and years.

Desert life

Cape ground squirrels live in the Kalahari Desert. They keep cool in the hot sun by using their big, fluffy tails as sun umbrellas.

When I use my tail like this, I'm much cooler. I can *be* in the shade wherever I go in the desert!

Cosy cactus

Elf owls are very small birds. They live in the desert and nest in giant cacti, in holes left by woodpeckers. The owls come out of the cacti at night to look for moths, beetles and centipedes to eat.

I lay my eggs inside this cactus. This helps to keep them safe from predators, such as snakes and **bobcats**.

Giant cacti can grow as tall as ten people.

My store of water stops me from drying out!

Desert burrow

This water-holding frog's habitat is the desert. In very dry weather it sleeps in a cool burrow underground. It stores water in pockets of its skin.

Ocean

The salty water of the ocean is the habitat of thousands of plants and animals, from tiny krill to massive blue whales. They live in different parts of the ocean, from the open water to the dark depths. The ocean is the Earth's biggest habitat. It covers around two-thirds of the surface of the Earth.

If lots of corals live together, they can make a coral reef.

The big blue

Sea turtles live almost all their lives at sea. Some may swim thousands of miles each year. They feed on animals and plants that live in the ocean.

Sea turtles only come to the seashore to lay their eggs. This is where all baby turtles are born.

Poisonous home

The clown fish lives in a sea anemone's (*say* see a-nem-oa-nee) poisonous tentacles. The anemone uses its tentacles to kill fish to eat. But the clown fish is covered in a special slime that stops it getting stung.

My microhabitat keeps me safe from predators!

In hot water

In some parts of the ocean, hot water rushes up from holes in the seabed. The water is boiling hot, but many amazing animals live in it. Crabs, shrimps and giant tube-shaped worms live in this microhabitat.

shrimp

crab

giant tube worms

Giant tube worms can grow up to 3 metres long.

Woodland

In woodland, many trees grow together. Animals and plants can live in different places in a wood, from the high treetops to the dead leaves on the ground. Homes in woodland are often shady and dark.

Some woodland trees lose their leaves in winter. Others keep their leaves all year round.

In winter, I **hibernate** in a cave or a hollow tree.

Among the trees

Black bears have long, sharp claws, which they use for climbing trees. They eat food they can find in the wood, including nuts and berries, and insects such as ants and bees. They also love honey. They scoop it from bee nests with their paws.

Oak mini-home

Gall wasps choose a special microhabitat for their eggs. They lay them inside the leaves and buds of oak trees. When the eggs hatch, the young gall wasps feed on parts of the oak tree leaf or bud.

oak gall with young wasps inside

gall wasp

An oak tree can live for more than 1000 years.

Rotten log

Fungi like to grow in damp, shady places. These fungi are growing on a fallen log. As they grow, they push through the log. They help the log to rot away.

Woodlice are small animals that live in cool, shady microhabitats, like underneath logs. They eat the old, rotten wood.

City and Garden

You can help by putting out bird food for us!

Some animals live in human habitats, such as towns and cities. Towns and cities have many different places to shelter, and plenty of **sources** of food.

Garden visitors

A garden can be a brilliant habitat for a hedgehog. Hedgehogs sometimes visit gardens at **dusk** to look for food. Hedgehogs eat almost anything, from frogs and worms to fallen fruit.

We can make our nests under hedges, logs or rocks. The nests are made from leaves and grass.

Chimney pot spot

White storks usually build their huge nests in trees. But sometimes they nest on top of chimneys and rooftops in towns and cities.

White storks build their nests from sticks, paper and rags.

Human Habitats

People live in lots of different habitats.

Some live in cities.

Some live in the countryside.

Some live in places
that are cold and icy.

Some live in places
that are hot and dry.

What is your habitat?

Glossary

bobcats: a type of wild cat with a short tail

cockles: a type of sea animal with a shell

dusk: just before the sun sets in the evening

fungi: plants without leaves or flowers that can grow on other plants; e.g. mushrooms and toadstools

hibernate: rest or go to sleep for a long period, such as wintertime

predators: animals that hunt other animals

sources: places where things can be found

wading: walking through water

Index

bears	23	oystercatchers	7
clown fish	20	sea turtles	19
crabs	8, 21	sloths	13
frogs	12, 17, 27	squirrels	15
fungi	13, 25	storks	28
hedgehogs	27	wasps	24
jaguars	11	worms	7, 9, 21, 27
owls	16		

Look Back, Explorers

 What is a habitat?

 Why are homes in woodland often shady?

 Can you think of one microhabitat in the book?

 Where does a clown fish live?

 Elf owls are 'very small' birds. Can you think of another word to describe their size?

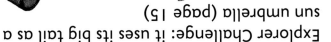 Did you find out how this animal keeps cool?

Explorer Challenge: it uses its big tail as a sun umbrella (page 15)

What's Next, Explorers?

Now you know about habitats, read about how Biff, Chip and Kipper help a sea turtle get back to its home ...

Turtle Beach

Series created by Roderick Hunt and Alex Brychta

OXFORD

Explorer Challenge
for *Turtle Beach*

Find out what happens to this shell ...